NEURALINK

MIND MERGE

Decoding the Brain-Machine
Interface Revolution"
Comprehensive Guide to fully
understand Neuralink"

LIBERTY PRIME

Introduction

"Plunge into the progressive world of Neuralink with 'Neuralink Intellect Merge,' a compelling investigation of the groundbreaking innovation that's reshaping our understanding of the human brain. In this captivating travel, find how Neuralink's imaginative brain-computer interface is bridging the crevice between people and machines, advertising phenomenal openings for upgrading cognition, communication, and network.

From the visionary intellect of **LIBERTY PRIME**, this book digs profound into the science behind Neuralink, unraveling its potential to revolutionize businesses extending from healthcare to excitement.

Through captivating narrating and master examination, 'Neuralink Intellect Merge' sheds light on the significant suggestions of combining intellect and machine, whereas moreover tending to the moral and societal suggestions that go with such transformative progressions.

Whether you are an innovation devotee, a futurist, or basically inquisitive about the frontiers of human improvement, 'Neuralink Intellect Merge' could be a must-read. Prepare to be motivated, challenged, and captivated as you set out on a journey into the long term of humankind."

Chapter 1:

Introduction to Neuralink

An overview of Neuralink, Elon Musk's groundbreaking venture aiming to merge the human brain with artificial intelligence. The chapter explores the potential implications of this technology on society and introduces the key concepts behind Neuralink.

Let's briefly explain Neuralink

Imagine a world where humans and computers are no longer separate entities but seamlessly integrated, where the mind can control machines and access information directly from the Internet

This may sound like something out of his science fiction movie, but Elon Musk and his team at Neuralink are working to make it a reality.

Neuralink is a company founded by Elon Musk with the ambitious goal of fusing the human brain with artificial intelligence (AI)

In other words, they want to develop technology that allows our brains to communicate directly with computers and other devices, without the need for a keyboard, mouse, or touchscreen

The idea behind Neuralink is to create a brain-machine interface (BMI) that connects the brain to external devices

The interface consists of tiny electrodes, thinner than a human hair, that are implanted in the brain

These electrodes can read and stimulate neural activity, essentially allowing two-way communication between the brain and the machine

How exactly does this work

Now, let's break it down.

First, electrodes are surgically implanted into the brain

Although it may sound scary, the goal is to use advanced robotics and neurosurgical techniques to make the surgery as minimally invasive as possible

Once the electrodes are in place, they begin receiving electrical signals from the brain

Our brains communicate through electrical impulses, which are essentially the language of the nervous system

These signals contain information about our thoughts, feelings, and intentions

The next step is to decode these signals and translate them into commands that the computer can understand

This is where AI comes into play

Neuralink's technology uses machine learning algorithms to analyze and interpret neural activity in real time.

For example, thinking about moving your hands generates a specific pattern of neural activity in your brain

BMI can recognize these patterns and translate them into commands to move a robotic arm or control a computer cursor

But Neuralink does more than just control external devices with your head

It's also about improving our own cognitive abilities

By stimulating specific areas of the brain, this technology has the potential to treat a wide range of neurological disorders, from Parkinson's disease to depression

Of course, with great power comes great responsibility

The implications of the fusion of the human brain and AI are far-reaching, both ethically and socially

However, there are also privacy and security concerns.

If our minds can be read and manipulated by machines, who has access to that information

And what happens if that technology falls into the wrong hands

Questions about inequality and access too there is Neuralink available to everyone or only to the wealthy elite

And what happens to those who choose not to enhance their brains with technology

Will they be left behind in a world where everyone else is augmented Despite these concerns, the potential benefits of Neuralink are undeniable

Imagine being able to learn new skills, communicate with others telepathically, and experience virtual reality with all five senses at the speed of thought

In summary, Neuralink represents a bold vision for humanity's future, where the boundaries between humans and machines are blurred and our minds are no longer limited by the boundaries of our bodies.

Whether this vision will become a reality
remains to be seen, but one thing is for certain:
the future of will be fascinating.

Chapter 2:

How Neuralink Works

A detailed explanation of the Neuralink technology, including how it interfaces with the brain, processes neural signals, and interacts with external devices. The chapter delves into the mechanics of neural implants and the principles of brain-computer interface technology.

Neuralink works by creating a direct connection between the human brain and external devices such as computers or prosthetic limbs

This connection is made possible through the use of small electrodes implanted in the brain

These electrodes are incredibly small, thinner than a human hair, and are used to both read and stimulate neural activity

They work by detecting electrical signals produced by neurons, cells in the brain responsible for transmitting information.

When we think, feel, or move, neurons send out electrical impulses to communicate with each other

These pulses create a pattern of activity that can be detected by electrodes

The first step in this process is to implant these electrodes into the brain

This is done through a surgical procedure that inserts a small chip containing electrodes into the skull

The electrodes are then carefully placed in close proximity to the neurons being recorded or stimulated

Once the electrode is in place, it begins recording the electrical signals generated by the neuron

These signals are sent to a device called Neuralink Link, which is implanted behind the ear.

This link acts as a bridge between electrodes in the brain and external devices such as computers and smartphones

It processes neural signals in real time and translates them into commands that these devices can understand

For example, when you think about moving your hand, electrodes in your brain detect corresponding neural activity

This activity is sent to Link, who analyzes it and translates it into commands that move the robot arm or control his computer cursor

But Neuralink does more than just control external devices with your head

It's also about improving our own cognitive abilities

By stimulating specific areas of the brain, this technology has the potential to treat a wide range of neurological disorders, from Parkinson's disease to depression.

Stimulation involves sending small electrical pulses to specific areas of the brain

These impulses can modulate neuron activity and increase or decrease the neuron's firing rate

This can have different effects depending on the area of the brain that is stimulated

For example, stimulating the motor cortex can restore movement in paralyzed limbs, and stimulating the hippocampus may improve memory and learning abilities

In addition to treating neurological disorders, Neuralink can also be used to improve everyday cognitive function

For example, directly stimulating parts of the brain associated with learning and memory may help you learn new skills faster

One of the biggest challenges in developing Neuralink technology is ensuring that the electrodes continue to function stably over long periods of time.

The brain is a highly dynamic and complex organ, and electrodes must be able to withstand constant movement and changes in neural activity

To address this challenge, Neuralink has developed flexible electrodes that move with the brain and can bend without breaking

These electrodes are made of biocompatible materials and are not rejected by the body's immune system

Another important aspect of Neuralink technology is the software that processes and interprets neural signals

This software uses advanced machine learning algorithms to analyze and decode signals in real time

Machine learning is a type of artificial intelligence that allows computers to learn from data and make predictions and decisions based on that data

In Neuralink's case, the software learns to recognize patterns of neural activity and translate them into commands that external devices can understand

Overall, Neuralink represents a breakthrough.

Chapter 3:

Advantages of Neuralink

Explores the potential benefits of Neuralink, such as enhanced communication, improved medical treatments for neurological disorders, and new opportunities for human augmentation and cognitive enhancement. Case studies and real-world examples illustrate the transformative impact of Neuralink on various aspects of life.

Neuralink offers a range of potential benefits that could fundamentally change the way we live and interact with technology

From improving communication to revolutionizing healthcare, Neuralink holds promise in many aspects of human life

One of the most important advantages of Neuralink is its potential to improve communication.

Imagine being able to send messages and have conversations without having to speak a word or type on a keyboard

With Neuralink, this can become a reality

By connecting directly to the brain, Neuralink has the potential to enable seamless communication using only thoughts

For people with conditions that affect their ability to communicate, such as: paralysis or locked-in syndrome, Neuralink can be life-changing

This may provide them with an opportunity to express themselves and interact with the world in ways that were previously not possible

Additionally, Neuralink could open new opportunities for people with disabilities to participate more fully in society

For example, people with movement disorders could be able to control assistive devices and computers with their minds, allowing them to live more independent lives.

In addition to communication, Neuralink also has the potential to revolutionize the treatment of neurological diseases

Diseases such as Parkinson's disease, epilepsy, and depression could all benefit from Neuralink technology

For example, Neuralink can be used to specifically stimulate certain areas of the brain to help reduce symptoms of Parkinson's disease, such as tremors and stiffness

By precisely modulating the activity of neurons, Neuralink has the potential to provide more effective and personalized treatments for a wide range of neurological diseases

Additionally, Neuralink may provide insight into the mechanisms underlying neurological disorders, opening new avenues for research and drug development

By recording neural activity directly from the brain, Neuralink could help scientists better understand how these disorders occur and how they can be treated.

Another benefit of Neuralink is its potential for human augmentation and cognitive enhancement

By connecting directly to the brain, Neuralink can improve our cognitive abilities in ways previously unimaginable

For example, Neuralink can improve learning and memory by stimulating the parts of the brain responsible for these functions

They may also be able to learn new skills faster by directly interacting with the brain's reward system and reinforcing desired behaviors

Additionally, Neuralink could open up new possibilities for virtual reality and augmented reality experiences

By stimulating sensory regions of the brain, Neuralink can create immersive virtual environments that are indistinguishable from reality.

Moreover, Neuralink could pave the way for new forms of human-computer interaction.

Instead of relying on traditional input devices such as keyboards and mice, we will be able to interact with computers and other devices directly in our heads.

Neuralink offers a variety of potential benefits, from improving communication to revolutionizing healthcare to enabling new forms of human augmentation.

Although there are still many challenges to overcome, the future is bright for this exciting new technology.

With further research and development, Neuralink has the potential to truly change the way we live and interact with the world around us.

Chapter 4:

Disadvantages of Neuralink

Examines the ethical, social, and psychological implications of Neuralink technology. Discusses concerns about privacy, security, potential misuse of brain data, and the risk of exacerbating existing inequalities. Offers insights into the potential risks and challenges associated with widespread adoption of Neuralink.

Although Neuralink promises to revolutionize many aspects of human life, it also raises important ethical, social, and psychological concerns that need to be carefully considered.

One of the biggest drawbacks of Neuralink is the potential for privacy violations.

By connecting directly to the brain, Neuralink technology could provide unprecedented access to our thoughts, emotions, and memories.

This raises concerns about who has access to this information and how it is used.

For example, imagine that companies and governments could collect and analyze data about our deepest thoughts and desires.

This can lead to serious privacy violations and can be used to manipulate or control people without their consent.

Again, there are concerns about the safety of Neuralink technology. What security measures are in place to prevent unauthorized access and hacking when our brains are connected to external devices Someone could manipulate our minds or plant false memories, It makes me very anxious to think that I might be able to do something like that

Another disadvantage of Neuralink is that brain data can be misused Like other forms of data, brain data can be vulnerable to theft, manipulation, and misuse.

This raises concerns about whether we can control how our brain data is stored, protected and used, and who has access to it

There are also concerns about the potential for Neuralink technology to exacerbate existing inequalities

If Neuralink becomes available only to the wealthy elite, it will widen the gap between the haves and have-nots, creating a world where only a privileged few have access to enhanced cognitive abilities and opportunities, there is a possibility

There are concerns about the psychological effects of Neuralink technology,For example, if we can expand our cognitive abilities through Neuralink, what does that mean for our identity and self-esteem, Do we rely on technology to think and function, or does technology help u.Will it enhance autonomy and self-expression.

Additionally, there are concerns about the potential for addiction and abuse of Neuralink technology, If we can stimulate the pleasure centers of our brains at will, what will stop us from becoming addicted to this artificial feeling of satisfaction.What safeguards are in place to prevent harm to others.

Additionally, there are concerns that Neuralink technology could be used for illicit purposes such as mind control and manipulation. If someone has access to our brain signals, they can influence our thoughts and actions without our knowledge or consent. There are concerns about the long-term health effects of Neuralink technology.

Although this technology is still in its early stages of development, the potential risks and side effects of implanting electrodes in the brain are still poorly understood. Can Neuralink technology cause unintended consequences such as neurological damage or cognitive decline.

There are also concerns about the social and cultural impact of Neuralink technology. For example, if we were able to communicate telepathically via Neuralink, what would that mean for our relationships and social interaction.

Will it bring us closer together, or will it further isolate us from each other, Is it ?

In summary, while Neuralink promises to improve communication, improve healthcare, and enable new forms of human augmentation, there are important ethical, social, and psychological issues that need to be carefully considered, It also raises concerns.

As we continue to develop and deploy Neuralink technology, it will be important to prioritize the protection of privacy, security, and individual autonomy, and to ensure that the benefits of the technology are equitably distributed across society.

Chapter 5:

Ethical Considerations

Explores the ethical dilemmas raised by Neuralink, including issues related to consent, autonomy, and the potential for unintended consequences. Examines different perspectives on the ethical implications of brain-computer interfaces and considers strategies for addressing these concerns responsibly.

A brief discussion of ethical considerations regarding Neuralink.

Elon Musk's plan to merge the human brain with artificial intelligence (AI) raises various ethical dilemmas that need to be carefully considered. A key ethical dilemma posed by Neuralink is the issue of consent.

For invasive techniques that interact directly with the brain, ensuring informed consent is paramount, Individuals are fully aware of the risks.

However, achieving true informed consent in the context of Neuralink presents certain challenges. This technology is still in its early stages of development, The potential risks and side effects of implanting electrodes in the brain are still poorly understood.

Additionally, the long-term effects of Neuralink technology are uncertain, making it difficult for individuals to fully understand the consequences of their decisions. There are also concerns about the potential for coercion and manipulation in the consent process. Do individuals feel pressured to undergo Neuralink procedures in order to keep up with technological advances or maintain a competitive advantage in society.

Vulnerable people such as people with disabilities or neurological disabilities, Are people disproportionately selected for experiments using Neuralink technology. Other ethical considerations related to Neuralink include issues of autonomy , the ability to control behavior is a fundamental aspect of human dignity and self-determination.

However, the introduction of invasive technologies like Neuralink raises questions about who ultimately controls our lives. For example, if someone gained unauthorized access to our brain signals via Neuralink, they could manipulate our thoughts and actions without our knowledge or consent This raises concerns about the erosion of personal autonomy and the potential for abuse of power.

Additionally, there are concerns that Neuralink technology may have unintended consequences. Although Neuralink's goal is to improve human performance and improve quality of life, there is always a risk of unintended side effects or unexpected consequences. For example, what happens when certain areas of the brain are stimulated. The brain causes unintended changes in personality and behavior.

Neuralink technology may inadvertently worsen existing mental illnesses or create new ones.

These are important questions that need to be resolved through thorough investigation and ethical oversight, In addition to these, we need to consider not only the ethical level, but also the broader social impact of Neuralink, there is. For example, how will widespread adoption of Neuralink technology impact social norms and values around privacy, security, and consent.

Will it lead to greater social cohesion and connectedness, or will it address existing deficiencies, Will you deal with it.

If only a wealthy elite had access to it, the gap between the haves and have-nots would widen, and we would live in a world where only a privileged few have access to enhanced cognitive abilities and opportunities. In addition, there are concerns that Neuralink technology could be misused for illicit purposes such as surveillance, mind control, and manipulation. If our thoughts and actions are monitored and manipulated by his Neuralink, serious questions arise regarding the erosion of personal freedom and the potential for authoritarianism.

Chapter 6:

Legal and Regulatory Framework

Discusses the current legal and regulatory landscape surrounding neural technology, including intellectual property rights, medical device regulations, and privacy laws. Examines the challenges of developing appropriate regulatory frameworks to ensure the safe and ethical use of Neuralink.

Let's take a quick look at the legal and regulatory framework surrounding neural technologies, including Neuralink.

The development and use of neural technologies such as Neuralink involves important legal and regulatory considerations that must be addressed to ensure the safe and ethical use of the technology, From intellectual property rights to medical device regulations and privacy laws, understanding the legal landscape of neural technology is complex and multi-layered.

One of the most important legal considerations related to neural technology is intellectual property rights. Companies like Neuralink invest significant time and resources in developing innovative technologies and rely on intellectual property rights, such as patents and copyrights, to protect their inventions and creations.

For example, patents give companies exclusive rights to their inventions for a limited period of time, allowing them to recoup their investments and preventing competitors from copying their technology.

However, navigating the neurotechnology patent landscape can be difficult due to the interdisciplinary nature of the field and the rapid pace of innovation, Additionally, in the context of neural technologies, there are ethical considerations regarding intellectual property rights.

For example, should companies like Neuralink have exclusive control over the technology they develop, or should they put mechanisms in place to ensure that the benefits of the technology are more widely disseminated.

Another important legal aspect is the regulation of medical devices. In many countries, neural technologies, including brain-computer interfaces such as Neuralink, are classified as medical devices and are subject to regulation by government agencies such as the USA.

Food and Drug Administration (FDA) and the European Medicines Agency (EMA), In the European Union. These regulations are intended to ensure the safety and effectiveness of medical devices and to protect public health.

Companies like Neuralink must demonstrate through rigorous testing and clinical trials that their technology is safe and reliable before it is approved for commercial use.

However, the development of neural technologies is inherently complex, and traditional regulatory frameworks are not always suitable to address the unique challenges of these technologies.

For example, how do you assess the security of a brain-computer interface that communicates directly with the human brain, What are the long-term effects of implanting electrodes in the brain and how can the potential risks be mitigated. Speed and agility of regulatory processes to respond to rapid technological advances There are also concerns.

As neural technology evolves and new applications emerge, regulators must be able to adapt and respond quickly to ensure appropriate safeguards are in place. Data protection law is another important legal aspect related to neural technology.

The ability to communicate directly with the human brain raises serious concerns about the privacy and security of sensitive neural data. For example, if neural technology can be used to monitor and analyze our thoughts and brain activity, who has access to this information and how is it used. How can unauthorized access or misuse of this data be prevented.

What security measures are in place to prevent this. Many countries have health insurance policies in place, such as the Health Insurance Portability and Accountability Act (HIPAA) in the United States and the General Data Protection Regulation (GDPR) in the European Union. There are laws and regulations that protect the privacy of information. However, these laws are not always sufficient to address the unique privacy concerns that neural technologies raise.

Additionally, the use of neural data involves ethical considerations, such as the importance of obtaining informed consent and ensuring that individuals have control over how their data is used and shared, There is a matter.

In addition to these legal and regulatory considerations, neural technologies also require broader societal impacts.

Chapter 7:

The Future of Healthcare

Explores the potential impact of Neuralink on healthcare, including its role in diagnosing and treating neurological disorders, monitoring brain health, and enabling new forms of personalized medicine. Discusses how Neuralink could revolutionize healthcare delivery and improve patient outcomes.

Let's take a quick look at Neuralink's potential impact on healthcare, Neuralink, Elon Musk's groundbreaking project, promises a huge opportunity to revolutionize medicine as we know it.

 By fusing the human brain with artificial intelligence (AI), Neuralink has the potential to transform the way we diagnose, treat, manage, monitor brain health, and deliver personalized medicine for a wide range of neurological diseases, I am

One of the most exciting opportunities offered by Neuralink is the potential to more effectively diagnose and treat neurological diseases, Diseases such as Parkinson's disease, epilepsy, and depression could all benefit from Neuralink technology. For example, Neuralink gives doctors direct access to brain signals and neural activity, enabling more accurate and timely diagnosis of neurological diseases. This may lead to earlier intervention and better patient outcomes.

Additionally, Neuralink has the potential to provide new treatment options for neurological diseases that are currently difficult to treat with existing treatments.

For example, by stimulating specific areas of the brain, Neuralink may be able to alleviate symptoms of Parkinson's disease, such as tremors and stiffness, and reduce the frequency and severity of seizures in people with epilepsy.

Additionally, Neuralink could enable a more personalized treatment approach by allowing physicians to tailor treatment to individual patients based on their unique brain activity and physiology.

This could lead to more effective and targeted treatments with fewer side effects. In addition to diagnosing and treating neurological disorders, Neuralink could also play a role in monitoring brain health and detecting early signs of neurological decline.

By continuously monitoring brain signals and neural activity, Neuralink provides valuable insight into brain function and may help detect changes that may indicate the onset of neurological disorders or cognitive decline. For example, Neuralink can detect subtle changes in brain activity that precede the onset of diseases such as Alzheimer's disease, allowing for earlier intervention and better outcomes for patients. Additionally, Neuralink could enable new forms of personalized medicine by providing doctors with real-time data about patients' brain activity and response to treatment.

This can help make informed treatment decisions and optimize treatment for individual patients, potentially leading to better outcomes and improved quality of life.

Beyond diagnosis and treatment, Neuralink has the potential to revolutionize healthcare by enabling remote monitoring and telemedicine, Using Neuralink technology, patients have the potential to receive real-time feedback and guidance from their healthcare providers without an in-person visit. For example, patients with chronic neurological conditions can use Neuralink to monitor their brain health and track the effectiveness of their treatments remotely, allowing them to more proactively manage their symptoms and avoid frequent hospital visits.

This reduces the need for Additionally, Neuralink allows patients to access their brain data and track their progress over time, empowering them to take a more active role in their health management.

This increases patient engagement and adherence to treatment plans, which can lead to improved outcomes and lower healthcare costs. In addition to its potential medical impact, Neuralink could also lead to new discoveries and insights into how the human brain works.

By providing researchers with unprecedented access to brain signals and neural activity, Neuralink has the potential to accelerate our understanding of brain function and open new avenues of research and discovery, For example, Neuralink could help researchers better understand the underlying mechanisms of neurological diseases and develop new treatments and therapies.

It may also shed light on fundamental questions about consciousness, cognition, and the nature of mind, Additionally, Neuralink will enable new collaborations and partnerships between researchers, clinicians, and engineers, potentially leading to interdisciplinary approaches to understanding and treating brain diseases, This could lead to breakthroughs with far-reaching implications for medicine and human health.

Chapter 8:

Transforming Communication

Examines how Neuralink could revolutionize communication and human interaction, enabling seamless communication between individuals, enhancing virtual and augmented reality experiences, and opening up new possibilities for collaborative creativity and expression.

Elon Musk's pioneering project, Neuralink, has the potential to change the way we communicate and interact in ways we never imagined. By fusing the human brain and artificial intelligence (AI), Neuralink enables seamless communication between individuals, powers virtual and augmented reality experiences, and opens up new possibilities for collaborative creativity and expression. There is a possibility.

One of the most exciting possibilities offered by Neuralink is the possibility of enabling direct brain-to-brain communication, Imagine being able to share thoughts, ideas, and experiences with others without the need for words or gestures, With Neuralink, this can become a reality

For example, Neuralink allows individuals to send thoughts and feelings directly to each other, creating a form of telepathic communication. This has the potential to revolutionize the way we connect with each other, removing language and cultural barriers and fostering deeper understanding and empathy between people.

Additionally, Neuralink has the potential to enable new forms of communication for people with disabilities or medical conditions that affect their ability to communicate verbally.

For example, people who are paralyzed or unable to speak can use Neuralink to communicate and express themselves through thought alone, allowing them to more fully participate in social interactions.

In addition to enabling direct brain-to-brain communication, Neuralink could also improve virtual and augmented reality experiences.

By connecting directly to the brain, Neuralink has the potential to create immersive virtual environments that are indistinguishable from reality.

For example, Neuralink can stimulate sensory areas of the brain to produce vivid sensations such as sight, hearing, touch, and even smell and taste in virtual reality experiences. This takes virtual gaming, entertainment, and social interaction to a whole new level, allowing users to be fully immersed in virtual worlds and experiences.

Furthermore, Neuralink allows individuals to interact with virtual objects and environments using only their heads, without the need for physical controllers or interfaces.This could make virtual and augmented reality experiences more intuitive and accessible, opening up new possibilities for creativity and expression.

Additionally, Neuralink has the potential to enable new forms of co-creativity and expression by allowing individuals to share and collaborate on ideas and projects directly from their heads.

For example, artists, musicians, and designers can use Neuralink to share each other's thoughts and ideas in real time and create artwork, music, and designs together in ways that weren't possible before.

In addition, Neuralink enables individuals to integrate their minds and collaborate on tasks and projects across traditional boundaries of space and time. For example, teams of scientists, engineers, and researchers can use his Neuralink to instantly share thoughts and ideas, accelerating the pace of innovation and discovery.

In addition to improving communication and collaboration, Neuralink can also have a significant impact on teaching and learning.

Neuralink has the potential to revolutionize the way we learn and acquire new skills by providing direct access to information and knowledge stored in the cloud. For example, students can use Neuralink to download information directly into their brains, allowing them to learn new subjects and topics more quickly.

Additionally, Neuralink has the potential to enable a more personalized and adaptive learning experience by tailoring educational content and resources to individual learning styles and preferences. Additionally, Neuralink can be used to improve an individual's cognitive abilities and mental performance through brain stimulation and strengthening.

For example, students preparing for exams or professionals looking to improve their productivity can use Neuralink to stimulate areas of the brain associated with memory, attention, and concentration, improving their ability to learn and perform complex tasks.

You can improve your ability to In summary, Neuralink has the potential to revolutionize communication and human interaction in ways we never imagined.

 From enabling direct brain-to-brain communication, to enhancing virtual and augmented reality experiences, to opening up new possibilities for co-creation and creativity.

Chapter 9:

Enhancing Human Abilities

Explores the potential for Neuralink to augment human capabilities, including improving memory, learning, and cognitive performance. Discusses the implications of enhancing human abilities through neural technology and considers the ethical and societal implications of these advancements.

Neuralink, Elon Musk's innovative company, has the potential to extend human capabilities in amazing ways. By fusing the human brain and artificial intelligence (AI), Neuralink technology offers the opportunity to improve memory, learning, and cognitive performance.

One of the most interesting things about Neuralink is its potential to improve memory. Imagine remembering every experience, every conversation, every piece of information you encountered, all in great detail. With Neuralink, this can become a reality.

For example, Neuralink improves the brain's ability to encode and retrieve information, allowing individuals to store and retrieve memories more efficiently.This gives individuals access to a wealth of knowledge and experience, which can lead to improved learning, problem-solving, and decision-making.

Additionally, Neuralink can also improve learning by helping you acquire new skills and knowledge more quickly and effectively. By stimulating specific areas of the brain associated with learning and memory, Neuralink may accelerate the learning process, allowing individuals to master complex topics and tasks more quickly. For example, students can use Neuralink to download information directly into their brains, allowing them to learn new subjects and topics more quickly.

Additionally, Neuralink has the potential to enable a more personalized and adaptive learning experience by tailoring educational content and resources to individual learning styles and preferences.

Additionally, Neuralink may improve cognitive performance by increasing attention, concentration, and mental clarity. By stimulating areas of the brain associated with attention and executive function, Neuralink may help people stay focused and alert in the face of distractions and cognitive fatigue. For example, a professional can use her Neuralink to improve her productivity and performance at work by improving her ability to focus and stay on task.

Additionally, individuals can use Neuralink to optimize their cognitive abilities for specific tasks and activities such as learning, problem solving, and creative thinking. In addition to the potential benefits, the prospect of improving human performance through neural technologies also raises important ethical and social implications.

When we think about the implications of using Neuralink to augment human abilities, we also need to consider what it means to be human and the potential risks and consequences of enhancing cognitive abilities.

For example, if Neuralink technology allows individuals to improve their memory, learning, and cognitive abilities beyond what is currently possible, what impact will this have on social norms, values, and inequality.

How can we ensure that the benefits of cognitive improvement are distributed equitably across society and that existing inequalities are not exacerbated. There are also concerns about the potential for misuse and abuse of this technology. If we could enhance our cognitive abilities through Neuralink, what would be the impact on privacy, autonomy, and personal freedom.

Preventing Neuralink from being used for illicit purposes such as surveillance, mind control, and manipulation Additionally, as Neuralink blurs the boundaries between the digital and physical worlds, we must consider its potential impact on the nature of human identity and consciousness. If our thoughts and experiences are expanded and enhanced through Neuralink, how does that impact our sense of self and our understanding of what it means to be human.

In summary, Neuralink has the potential to improve human performance in deep and far-reaching ways. From improving memory and learning to improving cognitive performance, Neuralink technology offers the opportunity to unlock new levels of human potential

However, when considering the ethical and social implications of using Neuralink to improve human performance, it is important to consider issues of justice, autonomy, and personal freedom.Addressing these concerns responsibly will ensure that you realize the benefits of Neuralink technology

Chapter 10:

Addressing Disability

Examines how Neuralink could empower individuals with disabilities, restoring mobility, speech, and independence through advanced neuroprosthetic devices. Highlights real-world examples of how Neuralink technology is already making a difference in the lives of people with disabilities.

 Neuralink, Elon Musk's groundbreaking project, has the potential to empower people with disabilities by restoring mobility, speech and independence through advanced neuroprosthetic devices. By merging the human brain and artificial intelligence (AI), Neuralink technology offers hope for significantly improving the lives of people with disabilities.

One of the most important ways Neuralink empowers people with disabilities is by restoring mobility.

For people who have lost the ability to move due to spinal cord injuries or other neurological conditions, Neuralink could offer new hope for regaining movement and independence.

For example, Neuralink allows individuals to control robotic limbs and exoskeletons directly with their minds, bypassing areas of spinal cord injury and allowing them to move and interact with their environments in new ways. This could significantly improve the quality of life for people with movement disorders, allowing them to carry out daily activities and participate more fully in society.

Additionally, Neuralink can also restore language to people who have lost the ability to speak due to diseases such as ALS or stroke. By decoding the neural signals involved in speech production, Neuralink could potentially allow individuals to communicate through computers and other devices simply by thinking what they want to say.

For example, Neuralink technology has the potential to convert patterns of brain activity associated with speech into text or synthetic speech in real time, allowing individuals to express themselves and communicate more effectively with others. This could give people with language disabilities a voice, help them maintain social connections, and enable them to participate more fully in their communities.

Additionally, Neuralink has the potential to increase the independence of people with disabilities by allowing them to more easily control devices and interact with their environments. For example, a person with paralysis will be able to use her Neuralink to smartly control her devices, computers, and assistive technologies in her home with just a thought and live more independently and autonomously.

In addition to these potential benefits, there are already real-world examples of how Neuralink technology is changing the lives of people with disabilities.

For example, researchers have demonstrated using brain-computer interfaces to restore movement to people with paralysis, allowing them to control robot limbs with their heads, drink water from a cup, feed themselves, etc.

We have demonstrated that it is possible to perform tasks such as Additionally, clinical trials are underway to test the safety and effectiveness of Neuralink technology in restoring mobility, language, and independence to people with disabilities. These trials are an important step forward in bringing Neuralink technology out of the lab and into the real world, where it can make a tangible difference in the lives of those who need it most.

In summary, Neuralink has the potential to empower people with disabilities by restoring mobility, speech, and independence through an advanced neuroprosthetic device.

By decoding neural signals associated with movement and communication, Neuralink can enable individuals to control devices and interact with their environments using only their thoughts, giving them greater freedom and autonomy in their daily lives.

As research and development advances, the future looks brighter for people with disabilities thanks to the promising Neuralink technology

Chapter 11:

Societal Impacts

Discusses the broader societal implications of Neuralink, including its potential to reshape work, education, entertainment, and social interaction. Explores how Neuralink could contribute to economic and cultural shifts and considers strategies for ensuring equitable access to neural technology.

Neuralink, Elon Musk's pioneering company, has the potential to reshape many aspects of society, including work, education, entertainment, and social interaction.By merging the human brain and artificial intelligence (AI), Neuralink could contribute to economic and cultural change and raise important questions about equal access to neural technologies.

One of the most significant social impacts of Neuralink is its potential to reshape work. As Neuralink technology becomes more sophisticated and widespread, it could lead to the automation of certain tasks and the creation of new job opportunities.

For example, Neuralink can help individuals perform tasks more efficiently by improving their cognitive and processing abilities. This could lead to the creation of new roles that leverage the unique capabilities of Neuralink technology, such as brain-computer interface specialists and neural data analysts.

Additionally, Neuralink has the potential to enable new forms of collaboration and communication in the workplace. By facilitating direct brain-to-brain communication, Neuralink makes it easy for teams to share ideas and collaborate on projects in real-time, regardless of physical distance.

Additionally, Neuralink could have a significant impact on education. Neuralink has the potential to revolutionize the way students learn and acquire new skills by giving them direct access to information and knowledge stored in the cloud. For example, students can use Neuralink to download information directly into their brains, allowing them to learn new subjects and topics more quickly.

Additionally, Neuralink has the potential to enable a more personalized and adaptive learning experience by tailoring educational content and resources to individual learning styles and preferences. In addition to its impact on work and education, Neuralink could also revolutionize entertainment and social interaction.

By improving virtual and augmented reality experiences, Neuralink can create immersive worlds and experiences that blur the line between reality and fantasy.

For example, Neuralink can stimulate sensory areas of the brain to produce vivid sensations such as sight, hearing, touch, and even smell and taste in virtual reality experiences. This could take gaming, entertainment, and social interaction to a whole new level, allowing users to become fully immersed in virtual worlds and experiences.

Furthermore, Neuralink allows individuals to interact with virtual objects and environments using only their heads, without the need for physical controllers or interfaces. This could make virtual and augmented reality experiences more intuitive and accessible, opening up new possibilities for creativity and expression.

Furthermore, Neuralink has the potential to contribute to economic and cultural change by driving innovation and creating new industries and markets. For example, the development and commercialization of Neuralink technology may lead to the emergence of new companies, products, and services that take advantage of the unique capabilities of neural interfaces.

Additionally, Neuralink may lead to changes in cultural attitudes and values regarding technology, privacy, and human improvement. As neural technologies become more integrated into everyday life, society may need to address important questions regarding privacy, consent, and the ethical use of neural data.

In addition to its potential benefits, Neuralink also raises important questions regarding equal access to neural technologies. Like any innovative technology, Neuralink risks exacerbating existing inequalities and creating new barriers to access for marginalized communities.

For example, if Neuralink technology is only available to a wealthy elite, the gap between the haves and have-nots could widen, creating a world where only a privileged few have access to enhanced cognitive abilities and opportunities.

Additionally, there are concerns about the potential for Neuralink technology to be misused for illicit purposes such as surveillance, mind control, and manipulation

When our thoughts and actions are monitored and manipulated through his Neuralink, serious questions arise about the erosion of personal freedom and the potential for abuse of power.

Chapter 12:

Navigating the Future

Concludes with reflections on the complex and multifaceted nature of Neuralink's impact on society. Encourages readers to engage critically with the opportunities and challenges posed by neural technology and to participate in shaping a future where the potential of Neuralink is realized responsibly and ethically.

As we think about the future of Neuralink and its impact on society, it is important to recognize that the path forward is complex and multifaceted. Neuralink has the potential to revolutionize healthcare, communication, work, education, entertainment, and social interaction, but it also presents significant challenges and ethical considerations that must be addressed.

 One of the most important considerations for the future of Neuralink is the need to critically examine the opportunities and challenges that neural technology presents.

Neuralink holds great promise for improving human health and increasing our capabilities, but it also raises important questions about privacy, consent, justice, and the ethical use of technology. For example, when considering the potential benefits of Neuralink for the diagnosis and treatment of neurological diseases, we also need to consider who will have access to this technology and who will bear the costs.

Will Neuralink be accessible to all, regardless of socio-economic status, or will it widen existing inequalities and create new barriers to access for marginalized communities.

As Neuralink enables new forms of communication and interaction, the implications for privacy and autonomy must also be considered. If our thoughts and brain activity can be monitored and analyzed through Neuralink, how can individuals take control of their neural data and ensure that it is used responsibly and ethically

As Neuralink reshapes the way we work, learn and interact with technology, we must also consider its potential impact on employment, education and social cohesion. Will Neuralink automate certain tasks and eliminate workers, or will it create new opportunities for innovation and collaboration.

In addition to these challenges, there are also important ethical considerations associated with the use of Neuralink for cognitive enhancement and human augmentation. While Neuralink has the potential to improve our cognitive abilities and improve our quality of life, it also raises questions about what it means to be human and the potential for unintended consequences.

For example, if Neuralink technology allows individuals to improve their cognitive abilities beyond levels currently possible, how will this impact social norms, values, and inequalities.

Cognitive Function   Additionally, as Neuralink blurs the boundaries between the digital and physical worlds, how can we ensure that the benefits of improvement are distribute equitably across society and do not exacerbate existing inequalities.

 The potential for misuse and abuse must also be considered. How can we prevent Neuralink from being used for surveillance, mind control, and manipulation, and ensure that it is used responsibly and ethically

 In summary, how to navigate your future with Neuralink, The opportunities and challenges of neural technologies need to be seriously addressed. Neuralink holds great promise for improving human health and increasing our capabilities, but it also raises important questions about privacy, justice, autonomy, and the ethical use of technology.

 As we move forward, it is important to involve a diverse range of stakeholders, including policymakers, regulators, ethicists, medical professionals, engineers, and the public in discussions about the future of Neuralink is

Develop regulations, policies and practices that promote the responsible and ethical use of neural technologies by considering a range of perspectives and values, ensuring that the potential of Neuralink is realized in a way that benefits all humanity,

www.ingramcontent.com/pod-product-compliance
Lightning Source LLC
LaVergne TN
LVHW051613050326
832903LV00033B/4477